NATURE CLUB

FOSSIL DETECTIVE

JOYCE POPE

Illustrated by
CHRIS FORSEY

EAGLE BOOKS

Published by Eagle Books
A division of Quarto Publishing plc
The Old Brewery
6 Blundell Street
London N7 9BH
England

© 1993 Eagle Books

A CIP catalogue record for this book is
available from the British Library.

ISBN: 1-85511-044-X

Designed by COOPER · WILSON DESIGN
Edited by Kate Woodhouse
Printed in Singapore
by Star Standard Industries (Pte) Ltd.

Nature Club Notes

Though you may not know it, you are a member of a special club called the Nature Club. To be a member you just have to be interested in living things and want to know more about them.

Members of the Nature Club respect all living things. They look at and observe plants and animals, but do not collect or kill them. If you take a magnifying glass or a bug box with you when you go out, you will be able to see the details of even quite tiny plants or animals or fossils. Also, you should always take a notebook and pencil so that you can make a drawing of anything that you don't know. Don't say 'But I can't draw' – even a very simple sketch can help you to identify your discovery later on. There are many books that can help you to name the specimens you have found and tell you something about them.

Your bag should also contain a waterproof jacket and something to eat. It is silly to get cold or wet or hungry when you go out. Grown-ups are living things too, so you should not worry them. Always tell your parents or a responsible adult where you are going and what time you are coming back.

Though good fossils are often found in steep slopes or cliffs, remember that chunks of rock may crash down at any time. It is far better, and safer, to search among the pieces that have already fallen. If you find somewhere where there are lots of fossils, do not be greedy – take only a few, for once they have all gone there can never be any more in that place.

Contents

W   a fossil?

Fossils are the remains of living things preserved in rock. They can tell us about life of the past. They are formed when plants or animals are buried soon after they die. The soft parts of the animal, such as skin and muscle, are usually eaten by *bacteria* and other single-celled animals. Only the hard parts, such as teeth, bones or shell remain. The *minerals* from the surrounding area help preserve these parts and change them into stone.

▶ Geological periods are mostly named after places where rocks with particular kinds of fossils were first described. For example, Devonian rocks were first found in Devon, so rocks with similar fossils in other parts of the world are always called Devonian. The periods are grouped into three Eras: Palaeozoic, Mesozoic and Caenozoic.

Sea-living creatures are the most likely animals to be fossilized. Usually conditions are not right for fossilizing all

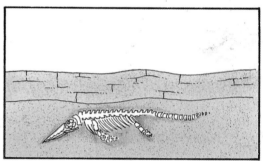

the animals that lived together. Here only the remains of the ichthyosaur survive. Its skeleton is quickly covered by silt.

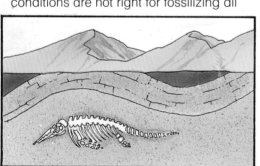

Gradually, minerals work their way into the skeleton to preserve it, while the silt hardens into rock. Over the centuries,

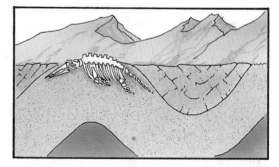

earth movement and erosion cause the rocks in which the fossil is buried to come to the surface. Then it may be discovered by geologists – or by you.

Most fossils are formed from creatures that once lived in water. These creatures sink to the seabed or river bottom when they die and are soon covered with silt. Fossils are usually the remains of animals without backbones, because in any environment these make up the majority of living things.

Most fossils are millions of years old, because they take a very long time to form. *Geologists* date them by seeing which fossils were in different layers of rock. The fossils in lower layers would be older than the fossils in layers above. Today geologists also search rocks for radioactive minerals, which help them to work out the age of the rock and, therefore, the age of the fossil.

Archaeopteryx, the first bird, is a Jurassic fossil.

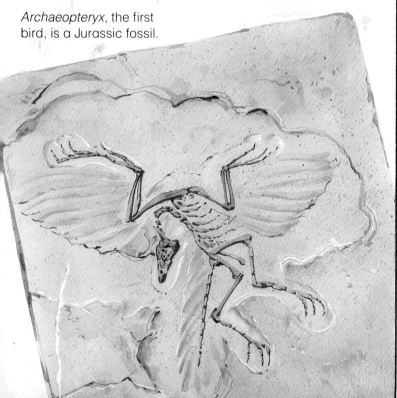

Holocene		
Pleistocene		Caenozoic
Pliocene		
Miocene		
Oligocene		
Eocene		
Palaeocene		
Cretaceous		
Jurassic		Mesozoic
Triassic		
Permian		
Carboniferous		
Devonian		
Silurian		Palaeozoic
Ordovician		
Cambrian		
Precambrian		

How to look for fossils

A fossil detective has to know about the different kinds of rocks. Some, such as those made from a volcanic eruption, hardly ever contain fossils, because any living things are destroyed by the heat of a volcano. But the silt and sand carried by ancient rivers made rocks that often included the remains of plants and animals. They are called *sedimentary rocks*. They are easy to recognize because they are layers of rock formed of grains of one size.

If you are a fossil detective, be alert when you come across sedimentary rocks. Any of them may contain fossils. You are most likely to find them where the surface of the ground has been cut by a river carving a valley, or where the sea has formed a cliff. Keep away from the cliff face, for even a pebble falling from above could injure you badly.

▲ A geological map is a great help when you are planning a fossil-hunting expedition. It shows where different kinds of rocks outcrop, or occur at the surface of the ground. Different sorts of fossils are found in each kind of rock.

▼ If you look at a piece of granite you will see that it is made up of minerals of various sizes that lie at different angles to each other, like a three-dimensional jigsaw puzzle. Sandstone, like all sedimentary rocks, is formed of layers of similar sized fragments.

granite

sandstone

▼ Beaches are often good places to look for fossils, but you should not hunt for them too close to the base of a cliff, where you would be in danger from falling stones.

Look out on the beach, and you will often find that the sea has washed and sorted the fossils. Groups of shells or sharks' teeth may be lying neatly together where the waves have left them.

Many parts of the world have been surveyed by geologists. It is often possible to get maps showing the kinds of rocks across the country. These can help you decide on the best places to look for fossils. Check the geological maps before you go on holiday: they can save you from searching for fossils in unsuitable places.

Making a fossil collection

You will probably start your fossil collection by chance. Maybe you'll notice an interesting or beautiful specimen when you are out walking or on the beach. Soon you will be looking for others, you'll be surprised at how many you find.

When you become a real fossil hunter you'll need some equipment. Most fossils are found in open country, so you must have proper footgear and clothes to protect you against the weather. Your expedition may last all day, so you'll need food and something to drink. Don't forget to take suntan lotion and insect repellent. And always bring a notebook and pencil or pen to jot down your findings. They can all be put in a rucksack, which will be useful for carrying your fossils home.

In some places fossils have been exposed by years of wind and rain, and all you need to do is pick them up. Generally, though, you have to remove them from the rock. In some soft rocks you can use a trowel, but most rocks are

▲ A hand lens is useful to see the details of what you have found. Wear it round your neck so that you won't lose it.

▼ A geological hammer and chisel will enable you to remove fossils from hard rocks. A trowel and brushes are best for soft sands and clays. Your map will tell you what sort of rock you should expect to find.

different sized brushes

geological hammer

broad chisel

small chisel

hard and you need a hammer. A geologist's
hammer is made of special toughened steel
that won't shatter when you hit hard rocks
with it. Small chisels are often useful for
getting delicate specimens from the rock.
Always wear glasses or goggles to protect your
eyes from flying pieces of rock.

When you collect fossils, take a few minutes
to note exactly where you found them. It's
sometimes difficult to remember the details
when you get home. Wrap each specimen you
find in a piece of paper – old newspaper will
do – or the specimens will jostle and damage
each other in your rucksack. Make a note or
write a number for each item on its wrapping
paper.

wrapped
specimen

fern fossil

ammonite fossil

goggles

small trowel

9

Your fossil collection at home

When you get your fossils home, you'll need plenty of space on a big table to unpack your finds. Until you've had a chance to look at and number each specimen, keep it with its wrapping paper. Then label it and put it in a small tray for storage. At first you'll probably be able to keep your collection in a small box, but soon you'll need more space. A cupboard with lots of shelves is best.

You need to be able to look at your fossils closely to study them. Before you can do this, you often need to remove some of the surrounding rock. Very small chisels or darning needles are the best tools for this job, but you have to be careful not to damage the specimen you're trying to improve. A hand lens is most useful for showing the details of a shell or tooth. You rarely need to use a microscope.

▲ ▼ If your day's fossil hunting was in rocks laid down in the sea centuries ago, there may be a lamp shell or shark's tooth in your haul. These often need little cleaning.

▼ As your collection of fossils grows, you have to decide whether to keep specimens from one place together, or whether to group fossils of one kind of animal or plant in each storage unit.

► Fine chisels, probes and even a paintbrush are useful cleaning tools. Make sure the specimens are dry before you put them away.

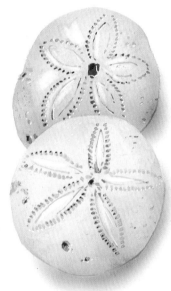

▲ These sea urchin fossils are similar, but different in detail. Your records should tell you whether they came from the same place, or whether they lived in different places and at different times.

There are many books that will help you identify fossils. But even if you can't name a specimen exactly, you'll find that almost all fossils are related to creatures alive today. You'll recognize snail-like creatures, starfish, lamp shells and many others. If you're lucky, you might find part of a backboned animal.

◄ A mounted lens will help you to see what you are doing so that you do not damage your fossils while you are cleaning them. It will also show you details of the specimens.

11

What fossils can tell us

The first thing a fossil tells us is that a creature of its kind lived in the distant past. But it often gives lots of other information as well. For instance, some kinds of creatures, like sea urchins and starfish, can live only in the sea. So if you discover a sea urchin fossil, you'll know that the place where you found it was once covered by the sea. You could find a sea fossil 800 kilometres from the present-day sea or 2,000 metres above today's sea level. Such a fossil tells you that the land and sea can change places. This has happened many times, and fossils chart the changes.

mammoth tooth

▲ Mammoth teeth are often found in gravel beds formed during the Ice Age. A single tooth may weigh 4 kilograms.

▼ 100 million years ago dinosaurs could walk from one continent to another.

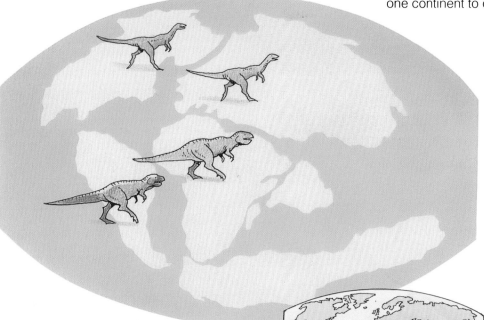

map of the world 100 million years ago

map of the world today

12

starfish fossil

You may discover the fossil of a plant or an animal from a different climate. If you live in a cool part of Europe or America and find the remains of reef-building corals, these will tell you that the climate was much warmer at one time, because these animals need a hot climate to survive.

Geologists have studied these changes of sea, land and climate. They have discovered that some great changes have occurred in the positions of the continents. Over the ages continents have slowly moved over the Earth. This movement is called continental drift. The same kinds of fossils found in different continents show that some continents were joined at one time and not separated by oceans.

▲ Starfish fossils tell us where seas once covered what is now dry land because they can only survive in salt water. Reef-building corals need shallow, warm seas, so the climate has also changed.

galaxea

reef-building corals

thecosmica

lonsoaceia

Animals preserved intact

Rarely, an animal's remains are fossilized so that the whole creature is preserved. Usually this is because it was buried so soon after death that even the smallest animals could not eat it. As a result, the skin, fat and muscle of an animal changes into a coal-like substance, but it is still possible to see the shape of the animal. In western Canada there are some ancient fossils as fragile as jellyfish. In Germany, the bodies of ichthyosaurs stranded on sandbanks were buried so quickly by the shifting silt from the tide that they were totally fossilized. We can see their dolphin-like tails and the fins on their backs, which we never would have seen if just their skeletons were preserved.

▲ Amber is a fossilized gum formed by various kinds of trees. Insects or spiders were trapped as the gum flowed from the tree trunk. The animal's outer skin is perfectly preserved, so we can see details of its eyes and legs.
▼ The most complete woolly mammoth known was found in Beresovka in Siberia, and is now in a museum in St Petersburg.

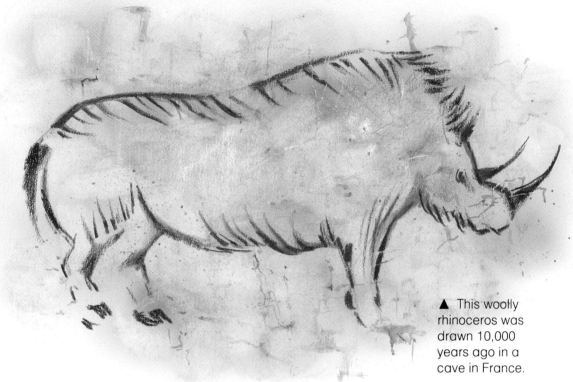

▲ This woolly rhinoceros was drawn 10,000 years ago in a cave in France.

▼ We can see this belemnite's tentacles and horny claws that helped it to hold its prey. Belemnites are related to squid.

In parts of eastern Europe, there are large amounts of salt and oil in the earth. When these come to the surface, they make a sort of pickling fluid that has preserved some animals. The largest of these specimens ever found is a woolly rhinoceros. *Stone Age* paintings showed woolly rhinos with a hump over their shoulders, which archaeologists did not believe existed. When the pickled specimen was found, the ancient artists were proved right.

The woolly mammoth is another Ice Age animal sometimes found complete. In Alaska and Siberia, these animals were sometimes trapped in frozen subsoil, which acted like a giant deep freeze. Even their stomach contents were preserved, so we know what they ate before they died.

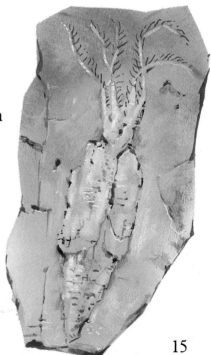

15

Fossil tracks and signs

The rocks you walk over are seldom smooth. One reason for this is that you are treading on part of an ancient world where animals burrowed and left their tracks. The tunnels of worms and other small creatures are quite common. These tunnels survived because they filled up with silt that was slightly different from the surrounding earth. When this soil hardened into stone, the burrows remained as wavy marks that stand out from the rest of the rock. Geological detectives studied these marks and have discovered many things about creatures that have vanished from the Earth.

Footprints are less common, but they have been found. They survive in places where the animals walked over soft mud that dried in the Sun before being covered with a new layer of sand. *Cheirotherium* is a fossil reptile known only from its chubby, hand-like footprints. Its

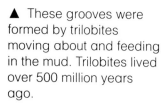

▲ These grooves were formed by trilobites moving about and feeding in the mud. Trilobites lived over 500 million years ago.

▼ When *Cheirotherium* lived, most of western Europe was desert. Its footprints in the mud after rain dried brick hard and were preserved in the hot weather that followed.

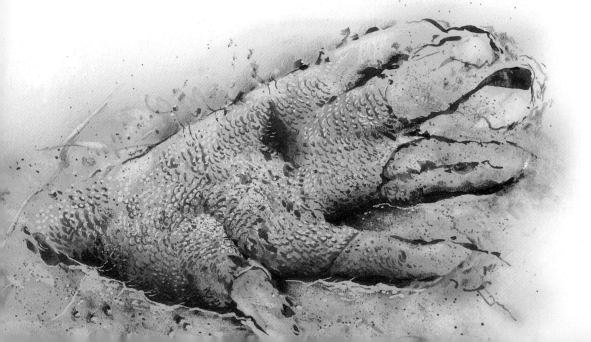

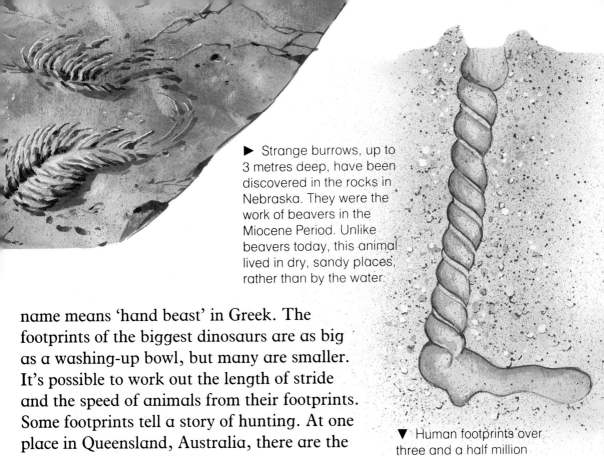

▶ Strange burrows, up to 3 metres deep, have been discovered in the rocks in Nebraska. They were the work of beavers in the Miocene Period. Unlike beavers today, this animal lived in dry, sandy places, rather than by the water.

name means 'hand beast' in Greek. The footprints of the biggest dinosaurs are as big as a washing-up bowl, but many are smaller. It's possible to work out the length of stride and the speed of animals from their footprints. Some footprints tell a story of hunting. At one place in Queensland, Australia, there are the footprints of 154 small dinosaurs, which stampeded across the mud flats at the appearance of a big flesh eater.

▼ Human footprints over three and a half million years old have been discovered at Laetoli in Tanzania. These footprints prove that our early ancestors walked upright as we do.

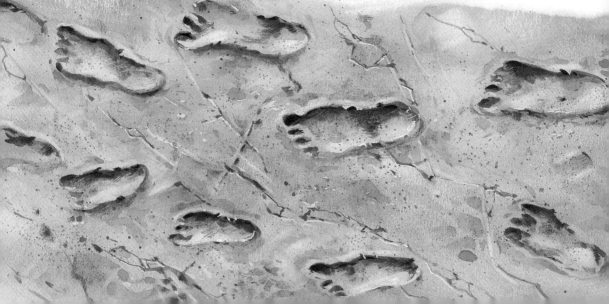

Fossil history

If you collect fossils from the bottom of a cliff or hill, you may discover that as you work your way up, the layers of rock change slightly. You may notice that the rock's grains are coarse and sandy at the bottom of the hill, while at the top the grains are much finer. This probably means that an ancient landscape has been worn down by rivers. In the beginning, the countryside was higher, and rivers on flat land usually flowed slowly. Slow-moving rivers carry only fine silt. You can see this today: mountain streams rattle with large stones, while lowland rivers wind muddily to the sea. Animals that live in sandy conditions can't survive in mud, so different fossils tell us how a landscape has changed.

In a few places, such changes can be examined in one area, but fossil detectives have to be prepared to find pieces of the puzzle spread across the world. The trail can be picked up and followed for a short way. Then

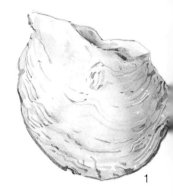

▲ Oysters used to live in rocky or sandy places (1). As their homes became muddier, those with curved shells survived (2, 3). The most curved are known as Devil's Toenails (4).

▼ Sixty million years ago the ancestors of horses were very small and lived in forests. As their environment changed these early horses changed with it. They became bigger, faster, plains-living animals.

hyracotherium   mesohippus   miohippus

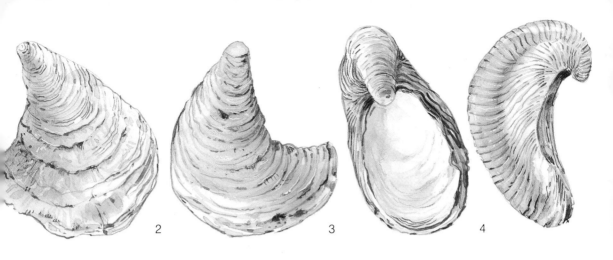

2   3   4

the trail disappears, and somebody a thousand kilometres away may find the next part of the story. People have been working to piece the history of life together for a long time, but there are still some gaps. Even junior fossil detectives can help to close these gaps by finding important clues in the rocks.

▼ Domestic horses differ from wild horses in many ways. After centuries of selection and domestication, many horse breeds are bigger and faster than wild horses.

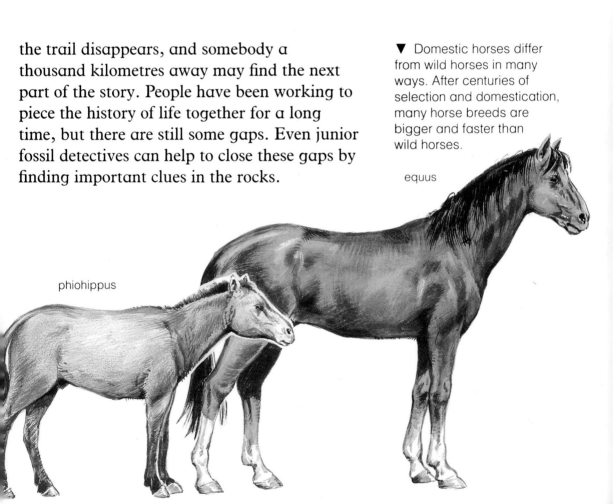

equus

phiohippus

The most ancient fossils

Geological maps tell you the type and age of the rocks in a specific area. The oldest rocks on Earth, which date back more than 600 million years, are called Precambrian. They contain very few fossils, and the fossil detective is unlikely to find anything recognizable in them.

Rocks of the Palaeozoic Era are likely to have more exciting fossils. These rocks are between 600 million and 240 million years old. In the early part of this huge span of time all plants and animals lived in water. In some places it is possible to find lots of fossils for in the Cambrian Period many kinds of creatures developed hard, protective shells. Most of these animals are related to present-day

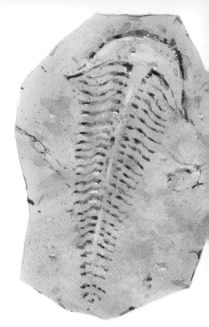

▲ *Spriggina* is a Precambrian fossil. By Cambrian times, all animals belonged to major groups that survive to the present day.

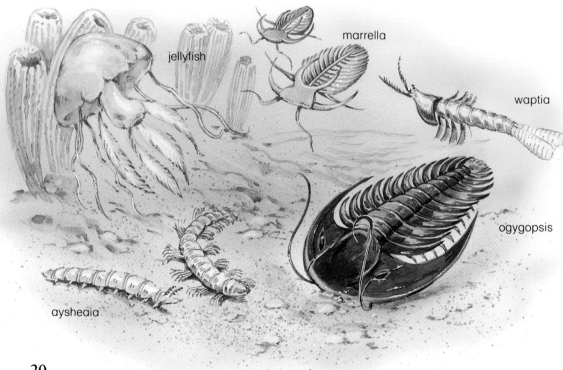

jellyfish

marrella

waptia

ogygopsis

aysheaia

creatures. A trilobite, for example, had a hard shell and jointed legs like a crab, a scorpion or an insect. There were also shrimp-, snail- and starfish-like animals, but there were no fish. The first fish fossils come from slightly younger rocks. They must have been unlike the fast swimmers of today, for they were heavy with bony armour.

Fossils that are about 400 million years old tell us that plants were beginning to grow on dry land. About 360 million years ago air-breathing creatures with backbones appeared on the land. Their descendants became the first reptiles. The forests they lived in would have seemed gloomy to us, because there were no flowers. The plants were like giant ferns and club mosses.

▼ Fish were the first animals with backbones. By the Devonian period, there were many kinds of fish. One was *Ichthyostega*, ancestor of the first land-living creatures.

Ichthyostega

Mythomasia

Palaso

Lepidocaris

Bothriolepis

The age of dinosaurs

The age of dinosaurs, or Mesozoic Era, began about 240 million years ago and ended about 65 million years ago. During that time dinosaurs were the most important animals, but there were many other living things such as crocodiles, turtles and the first mammals and birds. The first flowering plants developed during this time, so the world was becoming a more colourful place.

Although there were many Mesozoic animals with backbones, you are still more likely to find fossils of animals without backbones. You will probably not find more than a piece of bone or a tooth of a big fossil reptile. The dinosaur specimens in museums are the result of many people searching for over a hundred years. If you happen to discover a large part of a dinosaur, you should tell a local museum. It is hard work to remove a big specimen from rock, and it should be done by specialists with the right equipment.

mosasaur

Iguanodon

Megalosaurus

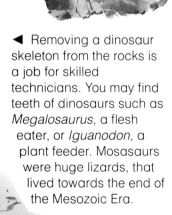

◀ Removing a dinosaur skeleton from the rocks is a job for skilled technicians. You may find teeth of dinosaurs such as *Megalosaurus*, a flesh eater, or *Iguanodon*, a plant feeder. Mosasaurs were huge lizards, that lived towards the end of the Mesozoic Era.

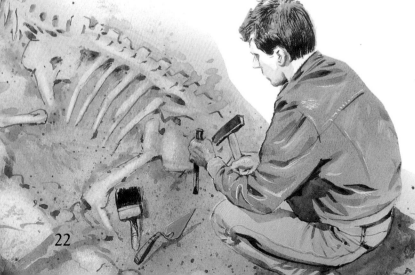

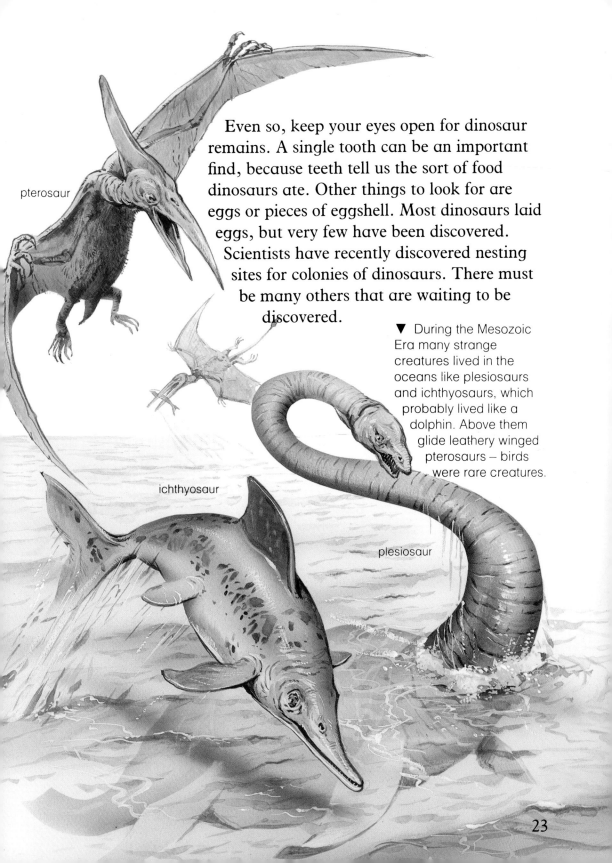

pterosaur

Even so, keep your eyes open for dinosaur remains. A single tooth can be an important find, because teeth tell us the sort of food dinosaurs ate. Other things to look for are eggs or pieces of eggshell. Most dinosaurs laid eggs, but very few have been discovered. Scientists have recently discovered nesting sites for colonies of dinosaurs. There must be many others that are waiting to be discovered.

▼ During the Mesozoic Era many strange creatures lived in the oceans like plesiosaurs and ichthyosaurs, which probably lived like a dolphin. Above them glide leathery winged pterosaurs – birds were rare creatures.

ichthyosaur

plesiosaur

The age of mammals

About 65 million years ago, the last of the dinosaurs became extinct. Just why this happened is one of the great mysteries of the past. There are many theories, but they can only be proved by finding more fossils, so there is plenty for you to do. Dinosaurs were soon replaced by mammals and birds, which are still the most important land creatures.

The great age of mammals is called the Caenozoic Era. Fossils from rocks of this age look more like the plants and animals of today. These fossils show us a huge variety of creatures. In the early part of the Era some birds grew very large. They were flightless and competed with the mammals for living space and food, but this battle was eventually won

Phororhacos

Diatryma

▼ Grasses were one of the most important plant groups of the Caenozoic Era. They provided food for many kinds of mammals.

▶ Giant flightless birds, such as *Diatryma*, lived in Europe in the Eocene Period. It grew to about 2 metres high. *Phororhacos*, from the Miocene of South America, was a flesh eater nearly 2 metres high.

► Brontotherium lived in North America during the Oligocene Period.

▼ Uintatherium lived in Western America during the Eocene Period.

Brontotherium

Uintatherium

Platybelodon

by the mammals. Today there are more than twice as many kinds of birds as mammals, but few birds compete with mammals.

Some Caenozoic mammals were as large as all but the biggest of the dinosaurs and many had huge horns and antlers. Many were closely related to mammals alive today, but there were far more kinds of mammals alive about 20 million years ago. The great age of mammals may be coming to a close.

▲ *Platybelodon* was related to the elephants. It probably used its bulldozer-like jaw to grub up the plants on which it fed.

25

The Ice Age

About two million years ago the climate began to cool down. Glaciers grew and covered the land. They left their marks in many ways, carving out valleys and transporting rocks and soil, for example. Water to make the glacial ice, which was often over a thousand metres thick, came from the sea. As a result, sea levels fell. You can often find *Ice Age* fossils in gravel spread by rivers that ran across the altered landscapes.

▼ This type of glacier can still be found in Alaska. It is carrying mud and stones, and rocks that have fallen from the valley walls. When the glacier reaches a warmer area and melts, the rocks it has carried may be many kilometres from where they were formed.

▼ Valleys with steep sides and a flat floor were formed by the weight of ice from glaciers moving slowly through them hundred of thousands of years ago.

As the weather got colder, many of the great mammals of the Caenozoic Era became extinct, but other kinds developed. These included the woolly rhinoceroses and woolly mammoths, which both lived in cold places close to the great ice sheets.

Some of the most important creatures were the ancestors of human beings. Their remains have been found in many parts of Africa. True human beings came more recently. Their bones are rarely found, but the stone tools they made are quite common in some places. Such tools tell us about the lives of these ancient people. They were hunters who followed the herds of horses, deer and bison across the plains of Europe and America. It was not until the ice had disappeared from most of the continents that people learned to be farmers and live in houses as we do today.

▲ These early people did not know how to tame animals or grow crops, so they had to follow the herds of wild creatures that they hunted for food. They made tools of chipped stone and of wood and bone, but they had not yet discovered how to use metals.

How to be a palaeontologist

A *palaeontologist* is someone who studies fossils. Few people are able to make their living this way, but many make it their hobby. Every year amateurs make exciting finds. You can know a lot about fossils even if you are not a palaeontologist.

You may be lucky and live near a place where you can find many fossils. But most of us have to wait until we go on a trip or our holidays. At other times, you can see fossils in museums. Museum curators are generally very helpful, and will show you how to find the names of the specimens you have collected.

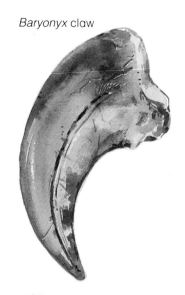

Baryonyx claw

▶ This dinosaur called *Baryonyx* was a dinosaur found by an amateur fossil hunter. It is often known as "Claws", because of the huge claws on its front feet.